Techniques to Rule the Stage: Pathways to Command Your Story Performance

by Leeny Del Seamonds

To Dirkje,
may your shining star continue
to shine — Live the Story!
＊
Much Love, Leeny

http://www.techniquestorulethestage.com
leeny@leenydelseamonds.com
Twitter: @leenydels

ISBN: 978-1508540953

Acknowledgements

Thank you to my family and my husband Grant for their unconditional support. Thanks to my editors for their expertise and diligence. I am grateful to Sean Buvala of Storyteller.net for his knowledge, guidance and encouragement. And special thanks to my gifted theatre professors and directors who molded me into who I am today. I am truly blessed.

Table of Contents

1. What is Storytelling and Why I Love it? An Introduction

Storytelling is the ancient art of relating a tale to one or more listeners through voice, movement and gesture. The storyteller looks into the eyes of the audience and together they tell the tale, bringing the written word to life. Storytelling is ageless and timeless and has no boundaries – it's existed since the beginning of recorded time and has, and will, span millennia.

Storytelling is a profoundly powerful tool to teach, entertain, heal and engage. It stimulates listeners' imaginations through vivid word pictures and physical expression without the aid of electronic media, immersing them in a language-rich environment. Storytelling enhances reading, writing, listening and interpretive skills and helps to augment the school language arts curricula through the integrated study of reading and storytelling. All of this is done live and in person, face to face: it's a soul connection.

We also find a reflection of ourselves in the stories we hear and tell, as we identify with – and evaluate – the story characters' emotions, values, challenges and triumphs, while taking the stories to heart. When we listen to stories, we are transported to foreign places and into multicultural situations which foster our understanding, appreciation and acceptance of human and cultural diversity.

Storytelling is the best vehicle for passing on factual information. Historical figures, social studies, geography and world events linger in listeners' minds when communicated in story form. Through stories, we are taught lessons in life, morals, language, culture, history, geography, science, math, the humanities, healing arts and the simple appreciation of human nature.

The storytelling experience can be profound and personal and is unsurpassed as a tool for learning about ourselves, about the ever-increasing information available to us, and about the thoughts and feelings of others. It also promotes a sense of community, as families and friends come together to partake in the extraordinary effect that stories have on us.

My journey into professional storytelling came through a stage door. Raised in a theatrical family who 'spoke story,' I studied acting, improvisation, voice, dance and mime. Armed with a B.A. in Theatre/Performing Arts, with a minor in Directing, I moved to the Big Apple (New York City) to make my mark. In between off and off-off Broadway gigs, I took additional classes in voice, acting, dance and mime. An actor never stops learning and growing in her craft. We know that in order to hone performance skills, we value the significance of researching, rehearsing and refining our body of work.

Although I love all aspects of theatre, I'm happiest when performing a tale. Through sharing a story, I'm best able to utilize mime, acting, singing, writing and teaching talents. As a story performer, coach and director, one of my favorite things is working with others who desire to learn these skills.

Together, let's **"Live the Story—*Vive el Cuento*!"**

2. Dressing up Our Characters to Bring the Story to Life

As little girls, my sister and I had a favorite game: playing dress up, a tradition that continued until we were preteens and beyond. We never grew tired of donning various outfits from our parents' discarded clothing and accessories stored in a large trunk in the basement.

I loved pretending to be someone else and was fascinated by the various components that helped me experiment in bringing a person to life. I'd create a mental scenario of who that individual was: rich, poor, smart, kind, trustworthy, mean, suspicious, ugly, or pretty. What did he or she do for a living? How did that person look and behave? What kind of gait and mannerisms did he or she possess? I pondered most about what type of voice this individual could have: high and screechy, deep and booming, soft and gentle, creepy, scary, melodic, loving, or perhaps silly.

Halloween was always a favorite holiday because my birthday is at the end of October. All my birthday parties were costumed events. Our costumes were never store bought. They were either sewn by our mother or grandmother or fashioned from various clothing pieces, hats, shoes, ties, belts, pocketbooks, and jewelry found in the basement trunk. And, with every homemade costume came a set of concocted character traits to complement the outfit.

My love of "trying on" different characters and pretending to be someone other than myself has been a lifelong passion and is, in part, why I became an actor. As an adult, I still love becoming someone else. In theatre, when a character is crafted for a play or musical, costuming plays a vital part and aids the actor in getting into the role of that character. In storytelling, the rewards are even richer: we often portray more than one character in a story. Storytellers don't stop in the middle of their story to don clothing pieces for each character being depicted, but determining what each persona may look like, sound, move and gesture is a huge step in creating unique and well-defined characters. It's like playing dress up, without the costumes and accessories. For me, this is fun stuff. I hope you'll agree.

This book has been designed as a reference guide to help develop your story craft over time. It teaches you how to get to the next step in your career and master the main stage with assurance and proficiency. I hope you'll refer back to it time and time again.

In the following chapters, we will examine and employ techniques and skill-building exercises to put you on the track to confident, proficient story performing. These topics include:

- Learning to care for and preserve your vocal instrument
- Exploring and applying a variety of distinct voices in storytelling
- Determining how to "stand in your setting"
- Researching and creating palpable story characters to breathe life into stories
- Discovering pathways to become a main stage performer
- Commanding the stage and taking it by storm!

3. Spoken Word Alive! Putting Your Best Voice Forward

There once was a Teller named Ben
Whose hoarse, tired voice had to mend.
A week off with REST
He learned was the BEST,
And GADZOOKS – he could tell once again!

Poor Ben! He made one big mistake: he waited until his voice was hoarse before taking care of it. By the time he stopped talking, allowing his swollen, abused vocal chords to rest and heal, Ben was in danger of damaging his voice and possibly developing vocal difficulties such as vocal nodules, polyps and chronic laryngitis. Fortunately, Ben learned that the best medicine for an abused voice is to REST it.

Losing your voice is no laughing matter. It is a storyteller's nightmare. This story can have a happy ending, if you learn how to take care of your voice. After all, it's the primary instrument used in your business, so recognizing the warning signs of unhealthy phonation is vital. Phonation is producing sounds with the voice. Some warning signs include having a dry, scratchy throat, sounding husky or gravelly, excessive production and presence of mucus and having a persistent cough. Don't wait until you lose your voice to care for it. Healthy phonation requires an ongoing commitment from you.

Healthy Phonation

The approach to healthy phonation is to prepare the voice to express – whether in speech or song – in a versatile, articulate and dynamic way WITHOUT STRESS. This is accomplished by proper use of the WHOLE body, through coordinated and/or correctional exercises. The whole body comes into play in the support and function of the vocal sound. Five important elements in creating a healthy voice include:

A. **Achieving proper posture**
B. **Diaphragmatic breathing** (controlled, supported breathing made by the action of the diaphragm)
C. **Relaxation** of the facial and neck muscles, especially the tongue and swallowing muscles
D. **Phonation** (making the voice well inflected and expressive and promotes a healthy larynx)
E. **Articulation** (clear enunciation when speaking or singing)

To better understand and apply these healthy vocal elements, invest some time to practice the following skill-building exercises to aid in bringing words alive and add dimension to your stories.

Exercise: Quick Stretch

Stand and slowly rotate head. Relax shoulders and arms. Shake out hands, legs, feet and rotate hips. Take two deep breaths: inhale and exhale slowly.

A. ACHIEVING PROPER POSTURE

1. Stand on both feet – one foot slightly FORWARD (3") and APART (4") from the other to achieve good balance. If feet are equally together, one must constantly adjust balance and hips will shift.

2. Allow your body's weight to LEAN SLIGHTLY toward the balls of the feet, with the toes lightly pressed into the shoes.

3. TUCK hips under and UNLOCK the knees.

4. SQUEEZE the buttocks ("pinch and squeeze" those glutes!) and STRETCH the muscles along the entire spine as far up as the neck. Stand high in the back. Don't raise the ribs in front, because stretching the chest upwards

tightens the abdominal muscles and reduces breath capacity.

5. RELAX the shoulders. Don't allow them to tense or rise upwards. Raise and lower shoulders several times to keep them relaxed while maintaining proper posture position. Repeat often.

6. Starting with both index fingers at center of breastbone, smooth an imaginary piece of TAPE horizontally away from each other across upper chest, allowing shoulders to open up and not slump. Pretend 'meat hooks' are at the end of the shoulder blades holding your arms. Relax and drop arms to swing freely as if each arm was a slab of beef. This helps to reduce tension in your hands and arms. It also trains you to maintain relaxed arms during performance.

When this posture is accomplished, hold position for a full minute as tightly as possible, relax and repeat proper posture position. Practice this posture exercise a few times daily. Eventually, this will become your natural posture for standing and walking, especially in performance.

B. DIAPHRAGMATIC BREATHING

Once proper body position is achieved, with spine stretched up, the rib cage will automatically be in an open position at the back. This position allows us to achieve controlled breathing for phonation (a voiced sound). The rib cage should not collapse upon exhaling. It is kept expanded by proper body posture, and replenishment of the breath is made by the action of the **DIAPHRAGM** with the help of the abdominal wall. Do not raise your shoulders or upper chest in front while breathing.

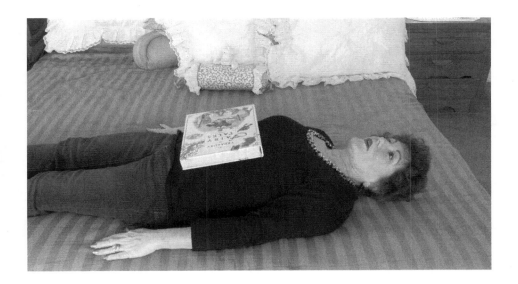

Exercise: Breathing from the Diaphragm

1. Lie flat on your back on carpeted floor or firm bed without pillow or elevated head. Arms should be

relaxed at sides and legs relaxed with knees unlocked. Place a large book (such as a hard bound dictionary) in the vicinity of the abdomen just below the ribs, where the diaphragm is located. Release any tension in your body. Take a deep breath, using stomach/diaphragm muscles to RAISE the book up, away from you. Hold your breath for three seconds then slowly exhale. You will be EXPANDING the abdominal wall as you breathe IN (the book should rise upwards) and COLLAPSING the abdominal wall as your breath goes OUT (the book should move back to original position). Your shoulders and chest should never rise up. With this technique known as diaphragmatic breathing, you will never use up all the breath you have taken in, and you will recognize the great control this gives you. Do this every day. Practice makes perfect.

Exercise: Strengthening the Lower Back (Optional)

2. Lean over, arching your back, knees bent, head down, and weight toward the balls of your feet. Take a deep breath and hold it. Come up on your toes and simultaneously pull the abdominal muscles in strongly. Be sure you are still holding your breath. Stretch up and down on your toes several times. You should feel a stretching of the lower ribs at the back. Eventually, this

will strengthen the lower back which aids in breath control.

C. RELAXATION

Once proper posture and breathing are achieved, fewer problems in relaxation will be encountered. Here are six exercises in relaxation:

1. Starting at the hairline and working down to the lower neck, gently massage the muscles of the FACE and THROAT. As you stroke downwards, allow the face to fall into a relaxed (or limp) condition. Rub the fingers over the eyes, closing them. Let the jaw hang relaxed.

2. Thrust the TONGUE out of the mouth, stretching it at the back. Repeat this rapidly several times until you feel less pull – then allow your tongue to lie over the lower lip. NOTE: The tongue is the one muscle structure most at fault, one which can prevent relaxation of the larynx and free emission of the voice. The tongue covers the entire floor of the mouth and extends down to the hyoid bone, from which the larynx (the organ of voice – it contains the vocal chords) is suspended. If the tongue is tense in any way, the singer or speaker will be in trouble because tension will also exist in the surrounding musculature that makes up the larynx.

15

3. This exercise is to relax the SWALLOWING MUSCLES. These are attached to the jawbone from its hinge to behind the tip of the chin and converge upon the hyoid bone from which the larynx is suspended. To relax these muscles, use the fingers of both hands to press gently, on one side and then the other, the soft part of the throat between the chin and the Adam's apple, starting under the hinge of the jaw. Gently massage these muscles until they are soft and pliable, moving the fingers gradually until they are directly under the chin. Place both index fingers together here. Swallow and you will feel downward pressure in the throat. It is vital that this area be kept relaxed, soft and pliable during all phases of voice production.

4. With relaxation of the other area in mind, take the LARYNX between the thumb and forefinger of one hand (or use both index fingers) and gently move the larynx from side to side to make sure it floats and does not click. A 'click' will indicate tension in the larynx or improper use of the voice.

5. Now take the CHIN between the thumb and forefinger and move it up and down, at first slowly, then rapidly. If the hinge muscles of the jaw are completely relaxed, this exercise will give you no trouble. The jaw should be able to move freely up and down without the slightest

resistance, while maintaining all of the relaxation you already have established. This is called the "chin-wobble."

6. To be sure that the LOWER NECK MUSCLES are relaxed, allow the head to nod up and down lazily while you are maintaining all the other relaxations.

D. PHONATION

A speaker must be aware of PITCH (intervals of sound tones, high to low), DYNAMICS (volume of sound, loud to soft) and RANGE (full extent of pitch, from highest to lowest vocal tones) to make his voice well inflected and expressive and promote a healthy larynx. Monotone speech is not only dull to the listener but can cause irritation to the larynx and vocal chords and can lead to vocal problems.

Years ago in Philadelphia, when I was directing students in a play, it occurred to me I didn't want to scold my cast members by yelling what other directors had done in the past: *"Speak louder!"* and *"I can't understand what you're saying – stop mumbling!"* So I coined the phrase **"Speak to Chicago."** There are three parts to my positive reinforcement method.

1. **"Speak loudly, but don't yell"** – Turn up your volume by imagining you're shooting your voice not only to the

back of the room but through the wall and across the land to another state. But by all means do not yell from the throat. If using a microphone, don't rely solely on it to project your voice.

2. **"Look up and out"** – Keep your face and voice up without talking to the floor. The floor does not have ears or interest in what you say. Listeners out in the audience want to hear and see you.

3. **"Speak slowly and clearly"** – Enunciate your words, taking much-needed breaths. Try not to rush and speak too fast, something new storytellers or speakers unfamiliar with their material often do. Articulation and clarity are key factors in successful speaking.

Exercise: Diaphragmatic Breathing and Projection

Place both hands on your diaphragm (at the base of your stomach) and practice breathing in and out. Do not move your shoulders up and down. Keep it nice and slow. After breathing diaphragmatically several times, practice saying *"HELLO!"* and *"MY NAME IS...."* while projecting your voice correctly across the room using the "Speak to Chicago" rules.

Exercise: The Yardstick, Inch by Inch Challenge

Think of a yardstick as representing your vocal RANGE, measuring the lowest vocal tone you can create, from the bottom of the stick, to your highest vocal tone at the top of the stick.   Every inch marker on your vocal range yardstick represents PITCH, the intervals of your sound tones – high, medium, or low vocal sound.

Point to the middle of an imaginary yardstick placed in front of you. Breathing diaphragmatically and 'speaking to Chicago,' say the word *"middle."* Repeat *"middle."* This is the middle pitch of your vocal range. It is your normal speaking voice and, for the most part, it's your narrator voice when telling a story.

Starting at the middle marker, travel up the imaginary yardstick by raising your pitch (inch by inch) as you say the word *"higher"* every inch until you reach your highest vocal tone. Return to the middle marker and travel down the yardstick by saying *"lower"* inch by inch to practice lower pitches. You should be pleased by the number of varied pitches your voice can make and will be able to apply numerous pitches when researching the best voice for each story character.

Exercise: Whole Body Motion/Emotion

This exercise reinforces self-expression and motivational techniques for solo expression. It combines vocal interpretation of carefully selected words with facial expressions, gestures, body movement and especially motivation (interpreting the word with inspired emotion). In interpreting each word, consider pitch, quality of vocal sound, or tone, use of dynamics and articulation. Remember: MOTIVATE, and then speak.

Looking in a mirror, or partnering with a fellow performer, interpret and speak the list of words below, one at a time. Remember: the **whole body** comes into play in the support and function of the vocal sound, so incorporate facial expressions, gestures and possible body movements to each word:

Happy, sad, delighted, miserable, ecstatic, elderly, youthful, evil, malevolent, pure, angelic, sneaky, frightened, strong, silly, serious, bored, boring, disgusting, outstanding, uncomfortable, awesome and unbelievable.

E. ARTICULATION

Clear enunciation is essential for every singer or speaker. It must become second nature for any successful performer through constant practice. The following exercises should be spoken first with clarity and enunciation, followed by integrating motivated emotion.

1. Which witch whooped wildly while watching whales wash?
2. How much wood would a woodchuck chuck if a woodchuck would chuck wood?
3. Merlin makes a magic motion with his marvelous magnet.
4. Buy your baker's best bread and biscuits.
5. Villagers vote to voice their views.
6. Have a heaping helping of honey, honey!
7. She sells seashells down by the sea shore.

Exercise: Interpreting the Written Word

Select and position several character voices while challenging your vocal ability. Use a digital recorder to practice vocal variety (pitch, tone, dynamics, articulation) by putting a voice to the following quotes:

"Well, what did you expect from a person like that? How many times do you need to be reminded? You never listen to me."

"You have made me so happy! My heart soars at the thought of being together again!"

"Mother, the pirate fell asleep and I was able to slip away. Look! I grabbed his pouch of jewels!"

"My loyal subjects, as your King I have served you well for many years. But now I must leave you. Farewell."

"Come here, young man, you must be hungry. Take this basket. Eat this food and drink this wine which I have prepared for you."

Bonus challenge: Now repeat this exercise using different voice interpretations. At the first reading, if you interpreted a character as wise, generous and patient, try the second reading with contrasting personality traits such as impatient, ignorant, greedy, and so forth. See how varied and diverse you can be when creating voices.

For a more in depth description of creating character voices, refer to Chapter 5, *"Breathing Life into Your Story Characters."*

Prevention of Vocal Problems - Strain and Hoarseness

Treat your voice with the same loving care a musician treats his instrument after a performance. When not in use, gently put your instrument in its case. REST your voice and avoid unnecessary speaking, especially on the telephone. Stay away from irritants such as smoke of any kind and exhaust fumes. Drink lots of water and avoid clearing your throat and

23

whispering. Laughing from the throat and excessive coughing may also cause harm. If you must speak, do it in a slightly higher pitch and lighter quality than normal. I call this using your **"Fairy Godmother voice."**

1. Your voice is a delicate instrument and should be treated as such. Protect it in winter and damp weather by wearing a turtleneck shirt or scarf. Don't take risks when it comes to your voice. Avoid yelling or shouting. If you must raise your voice, be extremely cautious and always support it properly through good posture, relaxation and diaphragmatic breathing. If you feel the urge to clear your throat, try a "hard swallow" after a sip of water instead.

2. Drink plenty of liquids daily (8-10 glasses of room temperature water is best), and carry a water bottle when using your voice for any duration such as a performance, teaching a class, engaging in public speaking, or attending/participating in athletic events.

3. Be sure to breathe properly and take frequent breaths when speaking. Don't make the mistake of chattering on, determined to finish a sentence or put the point across without taking those much-needed breaths.

4. Be prepared. To avoid stress, be sure you know your material before speaking, performing or singing. Embarking

upon a performance without knowing your subject well will certainly make you nervous and affect your voice adversely. Practice daily for a short while, to be certain of your material and your technique. A digital recorder is an excellent tool for learning material, as well as hearing vocal variety and patterns.

5. At the first sign of a strained, scratchy voice, STOP TALKING. Rest your voice by being quiet. Write notes if necessary. Avoid talking on the telephone for any length of time, and above all - DO NOT WHISPER! Whispering adds additional strain to the vocal chords. If you must speak, use your Fairy Godmother voice and speak in a higher, lighter pitch. This helps rest overworked, swollen vocal chords. Drink warm, soothing slippery elm tea such as "Throat Coat" by Traditional Medicinal Teas. Menthol can dry the throat and vocal chords, so use non-mentholated cough drops or plain hard candies to keep your throat moist and lubricated.

6. During the Holidays when inclement weather, increased social gatherings and added holiday stress can take its toll on your vocal chords, be sure to get adequate sleep and rest your voice. Laughing long and hard in a social situation is good for the soul, but can be detrimental to your voice if it is at risk. I'm not suggesting you can't enjoy a good laugh, but be aware that excessive, unsupported laughing from the throat can strain your vocal chords. A broad smile and a

twinkle in your eye can also get the point across - and is healthier for your instrument.

4. Live the Story! Stand in Your Setting

"Live the Story!" That's been my motto for over 26 years. You probably saw it in the first chapter, along with its Spanish translation, *"Vive el Cuento!"* I strive to apply this motto to my body of work as a performer and teaching artist.

As a story coach and director, I often observe students concentrating so hard on saying the words in their story they forget to "Live the Story." How does one achieve this? When spoken word is brought to life, several performance techniques come into play: incorporating healthy phonation and compelling vocal variety, applying motivated actions and gestures, portraying palpable story characters, believing in what you are stating and seeing in the moment, and standing in your setting.

"Live the Story" means you, as narrator, bring the story to life in front of an audience. As the tale unfolds, you believe what you're saying and witnessing as you relive the plot and invite the audience to experience the story with you. The audience wants to go on this journey to see what sights you see, meet the characters you introduce, and observe firsthand the action, plot twists, conflicts and resolutions of the tale being told.

The role of narrator is one of the most pivotal parts of the story performance. The narrator moves the story along, describes the setting to the audience, giving them a sense of place, and introduces the various characters as the story unfolds. Narrator is a vital component of the story and is definitely not an outsider.

Think of narrator as a conductor. He orchestrates, or arranges, the way in which the story is told. Like a conductor of an orchestra, narrator sets the story's tempo, dynamics, and rhythm. He may slow it down, or speed it up as necessary, especially if there's a potentially confusing part to the listeners. Narrator delights in tying the loose ends at the conclusion of the story, or purposefully leaves the audience hanging depending upon what type of story is being presented.

As storyteller, you wear several hats. You play the narrator and the many characters that enter your story and, hopefully, you will allow your characters to speak to one other. You, as narrator, also observe and describe the action as the story unfolds and sometimes – with a simple glance, smile, frown, or shrug to the audience – pass judgment or express an opinion, thereby influencing the audience's perspective.

In performance, as narrator, you walk to center stage to begin telling your story. It's important to immerse yourself in the story and be in the moment while telling the tale. One way to do this is to **"stand in your setting."** Using imagination and research you've conducted to create the setting, place yourself in the middle of the village, jungle, kingdom, prairie, marketplace, kitchen, forest, villa or desert of your tale.

As narrator of your story, determine WHERE in the setting you are standing. When you look around, you should "see" all the surroundings (buildings, trees, streams, castles, animals, people and so forth) that your setting encompasses.

Additionally, decide from which DIRECTION on stage each character enters and exits a scene in your story. In most cases, the narrator would gesture to that location when introducing a character and may watch that character leave the scene as she exits. Does the character enter from your left side (called stage left) or right side (stage right)? Does that character exit the stage from the left or right direction? Is the character coming towards you at center stage? If you are portraying two speaking characters with dialogue between them, I don't recommend one character enter a scene from behind you because when that character speaks, you (as the other character) may be tempted to turn around and answer or respond – which would result in your back facing the audience. That's never a good option.

For example, when adapting a Russian story about an evil witch ("Baba Yaga") and an innocent young girl ("Marina"), as narrator, I introduce Marina by having her enter the scene from stage left (coming from the dense forest). Baba Yaga is placed on my right side, where her run-down shack stands.

When Baba Yaga speaks to Marina, I become the witch and move my body a quarter turn to the LEFT towards the little girl and cry, *"Vat do you vant, leetle girl?"* Then as I transform, or morph, into Marina's character, I move my body a quarter turn to the RIGHT to answer the witch, *"If you please, my stepmoter vants to borrow a needle und tread."* As their conversation continues, Baba Yaga turns her body slightly to the left to question Marina, and Marina turns her body slightly to the right to respond. This way, throughout their conversation my face and voice will be seen and heard by the audience without being blocked, and the audience has a clear understanding as to where each character is standing.

As narrator, when introducing a character to the audience, you must totally believe that the character exists. If you look directly at the character, the audience sees her too. In many ways, the character becomes as real to the audience as it does to the storyteller. This is **"seeing is believing."**

The same principle applies to imaginary objects or props in the story. If we create something, it becomes real and it should show in our faces when we look at it. If we pick up an imaginary object and believe that it's real, the audience will agree. If we fail to put it down or ignore it, often the audience wonders where it went. Was the object dropped? There also should be the same level of motivated believability in the actions and gestures we portray in a story (such as running, climbing, pointing, jumping and so forth).

When blocking (adding movement to) an intricate scene in the Baba Yaga story discussed earlier, Marina is sent to the witch's kitchen to fetch a large pot, fill it with water from the well and place it on the stove to heat. During that scene,

Marina handles several pantomimed "props": a piece of meat, a pitcher of milk and saucer from the table, a large cooking pot and bottle of lamp oil from a tall shelf. Marina also encounters a cat and dog.

In deciding where all the props and animals should be, I drew a picture of the scenery, the same as a set designer would sketch a set in a play. I determined where the kitchen door should be for entering and exiting. Next to the door I placed the stove. In the middle of the small room I drew the circular table with the meat, pitcher of milk and saucer on it. The tall shelf with the large pot and bottle of lamp oil stood to the left of the table. Both dog and cat were placed lying on the floor next to the table.

When Marina enters the kitchen, she stands in front of the table, picks up the piece of meat and tosses it to the growling dog on the floor near the table. She then pours milk from the pitcher into the saucer and bends down to feed the cat in front of her. Marina looks up to the shelf on her left and sees the cooking pot and oil. She reaches up and first takes the large pot down off the shelf with her right hand, then uses her left hand to take the lamp oil and places it in the pocket on the left side of her smock (this 'pocket' was established in an earlier scene in her home). Then Marina exits the door on her right, still carrying the pot in her right arm.

As she reaches the squeaky gate, Marina takes the lamp oil from her left pocket. With her left hand, she shakes a few drops of oil on the gate's hinges, places the bottle of oil back into her pocket and walks on, with the pot still in her right hand. Marina arrives at the tall birch tree, stops and places the pot on the ground and removes a long blue hair ribbon from her left pocket behind the oil. With both hands, she ties a bow around the tree trunk before picking up the pot and heading to the well. In performance, this scene runs smoothly with storyteller/narrator describing some of the actions and props while using mime to portray the rest.

Not once does the audience see an object drop on the ground. If they did, because I carelessly forgot to put the 'prop' down, the audience could become distracted and may miss a key part of the story. Drawing a sketch of the scenery in advance of blocking the movement gave me a clear vision of how to maneuver this scenario and where to place the necessary objects.

Applying these performance techniques to "stand in your setting" not only makes storytelling more fulfilling for you, it helps create a closer connection with your audience. Remember to "**Live the Story – *Vive el Cuento!*"**

5. Breathing Life into Your Story Characters

An actor never stops learning and growing in her craft/calling. In order to hone performance skills, we value the significance of researching, rehearsing and refining our body of work.

How do you breathe life into story characters? By creating and presenting distinctive, precise, and palpable characters in the tales you tell.

As performers, we often portray multiple characters in our stories. But we certainly don't want every character to look, sound and behave the same. We want each one to be unique, individual and believable. To achieve this, it's essential to research, interpret and develop distinguished, well-defined and clear-cut story characters by approaching the character as an actor would approach researching and crafting a character in a play.

Having an appropriate voice for each character is essential. The whole body plays a vital part in obtaining and maintaining healthy phonation, in creating diverse vocal pitches and qualities, and in developing vibrant, specific character voices. Additionally, we use our bodies, hands and faces to enhance communication and frequently add gestures, movement and/or mime along with vocal variety to portray convincing characterizations.

Determining the story character's personality, motivation, physical characteristics, and how she moves, sounds, and conducts herself are all part of "breathing life" into story characters.

Character Development

In character development, there are 3 R's that should be applied: Research, Rehearse and Refine.

A. RESEARCH

Whether you are adapting a folk tale or writing a family/personal story, research plays a significant role in character creation and story setting. Conducting research requires good investigator skills and a well-developed sense of curiosity.

One of my goals, when researching and ultimately performing a multicultural tale, is to accurately replicate a character's accent and gestures. I strive to incorporate a selection of the foreign language into the story, thus maintaining cultural authenticity and avoiding stereo-typical caricatures of members of foreign cultures. When writing a personal story, research is equally key in precisely portraying believable characters, such as relatives, ancestors, real people and fictional personas.

The following resources may prove helpful with your research: libraries, anthologies, folklore collections, reference books, history and social studies books, museums, maps and atlases, abundant web sites on the Internet designed for storytelling research, movies from a particular era or country, computer CDs or DVDs, magazines and periodicals, and interviewing people (including relatives) from a specific country and culture. This is a personal favorite, but you may think of additional resources to gain knowledge and facts pertaining to your story and its characters.

Before analyzing and interpreting your story character, consider the following:

- Where and when does the story take place? What is the geographical location, date, year, season, climate, and time of day?

- What is the economic, social, religious and political environment?

- Is there a setting? Setting is significant to your story, especially when crafting unique, clear story characters. If this information doesn't exist in the traditional tale, adapt it by creating your own setting/scenery using various resources to make accurate decisions.

The next step in your research is to analyze your character's traits and personality. Every performer should answer three questions about each character he plans to portray:

1. **Who am I?** Define the character's personality traits, appearance, age, voice, and any unusual features or qualities.

2. **What do I want?** Determine the character's goals and objectives.

3. **What am I willing to do to get it?** How does the character attempt to achieve these goals? What is the character's motivation for doing what she does?

Make a list of adjectives to describe each character. Include personality, temperament, physical characteristics, abilities and/or limitations. Contemplate what others might say about that character. Is there a fatal flaw which is the character's undoing (such as greed, lust, vanity, jealousy, or desperation)? Find at least one redeeming quality about each character, one with which you can identify and ultimately justify why this character is the way she is.

Think about dialogue. What does the character say or think aloud? This is beneficial when writing or rewriting your character's dialogue, or verbal communication. Consider choice of words used by the character and her style or manner of speaking. When adapting a written folk tale, you may find there is limited dialogue in the tale. Often the narrator informs readers what each character is saying or thinking. In storytelling, we adapt that information and turn it into words for the characters to speak. This is my favorite part of storytelling: to give each character a distinct voice and write words they should be saying in their manner of speaking. It is more entertaining to the audience when the characters speak for themselves versus the narrator telling us what they are thinking or stating. This plays a large part in bringing the characters to life. It's enjoyable and rewarding to become the characters and speak for them.

Does the character have a dialect? If so, research authentic accents by listening to foreign language tapes or audio recordings by natives from a particular culture. Watch movies from a foreign country or one which features an actor with a foreign accent. Interview someone from a specific culture/foreign country and record accents, tempo and speech patterns to aid in replicating your character's accent.

Consider previous action. What happened to this character before entering the first scene of the story and what action involving the character occurs between scenes? Look carefully at the initial mood/intensity of each character at the beginning of the story. Determine where this character was before the story begins and what he was doing. Does this character change or grow during the course of the story? If so, in what ways?

Once you have gathered your character analysis information and personality traits, you can begin to define your character. Think about how each story character may look based on physical appearance, body stance, movements, gestures and facial expressions. How does this character sound when speaking?

Casting Voices for Your Story Characters

As discussed in Chapter 3, *"Spoken Word Alive! Putting Your Best Voice Forward,"* experiment with various voices to find the best one to suit your character. Be aware of PITCH (intervals of sound tones, high to low), DYNAMICS (volume of sound, loud to soft), TEMPO (speed and rhythm of sound), RANGE (full extent of pitch, from highest to lowest vocal tones) and ARTICULATION (diction and clear delivery) to create well inflected and expressive voices.

Finding an appropriate voice for a specific story character doesn't always come easily. Sometimes you need to tryout and test various pitches, dynamics and vocal qualities to discover the most suitable voice. A digital recorder is a valuable tool.

When researching my retelling of "The Tiger, Brahman and Jackal" folktale from East India, I initially cast the Tiger's voice with a loud, deep pitch and gravelly quality to match his natural snarls and growls. The Tiger would growl, then speak,

"Let me out of this cage!" and growl once more. The sounds of Tiger's growling flowed smoothly before and after his dialogue using one breath. After listening to this voice several times on the digital recorder, I believed it was an appropriate voice for Tiger and was content. However, I soon realized that every time I used this voice, I coughed and choked because it was difficult to sustain. This voice was clearly placed incorrectly in my range and could potentially damage my vocal instrument.

I was concerned that if I altered Tiger's voice, I might compromise some of his qualities and edge that brought his personality to life. Using the recorder, I experimented with different pitches (higher and lower) and dynamics (louder and softer) to find a healthier, but still apt, voice to use. What I discovered was by raising my pitch slightly higher and speaking slightly softer, I created an equally effective voice for Tiger without causing potential injury to my vocal chords. Plus I was still able to integrate the gravelly quality, snarls and growls with this higher pitch.

When casting voices for multiple characters in a story, preference is given to the amount of dialogue written for each character. I begin my research with the character that has the most to say. Once I create that voice, I move onto the character with the second most dialogue and using a digital recorder, select a higher or lower pitch than the first speaking character, keeping in mind its relevance to that character's personality. Then I apply vocal qualities, dynamics, tempo, rhythms, articulation or accent suitable to the character. I make good use of the recorder to compare and contrast those two voices. I proceed in this manner until all character voices in the story are cast. If the character is female or youthful, a higher, lighter pitch with a softer dynamic is often selected. If the character is regal and powerful, a lower pitch with a louder dynamic is used.

In casting speaking animal and bird voices, I try to match the same pitch as close as possible to the actual animal sound effect or bird call and incorporate those sounds with their spoken dialogue. This is exciting and enjoyable work and truly brings those characters to life.

Again, a digital recorder is a valuable tool to hear the differences in voice selections and aids in identifying one character voice from another. It also helps you detect **"voice bleed."** "Voice bleed" occurs when a storyteller retains hints of the same distinct voice used by one character and 'bleeds' that voice into what narrator (or another character) says next. In other words, if you use a gravelly voice in a low pitch when Tiger growls, *"I'm hungry!"* followed by narrator speaking in the same low, gravelly voice when he says, *"declared the Tiger"* – that's voice bleed. You want to ISOLATE each character voice and keep it separate from one another, especially narrator. Narrator is YOUR voice, not the voice of any characters you create. Rehearsing your dialogue on the recorder and listening carefully to yourself will assure you're keeping your character voices unique and separate from narrator.

Making clean, crisp delineation between narrator and characters helps to breathe life into the story and keep it tight.

A full-length mirror is useful in seeing what the character looks like, as you test various gestures, body positions, facial expressions, and so forth. Be aware of your hands when speaking — try not to repeat the same hand gesture or repetitive 'hand pattern.' Watch yourself in the mirror or ask a trusted friend or coach to observe you.

In developing more than one story character, use the character analysis research to compare and contrast qualities and personality traits of each one. Experiment with diverse interpretations of voice and body stance/position, making each character exclusive, exceptional and distinct.

B. REHEARSE

I am a firm believer in creating hard copies of my stories. It's highly beneficial to write or type your stories-in-progress because they become your scripts. Use this script to rehearse, make changes, keep notes and include introductions. Be prepared to edit your script several times, incorporating changes as you practice the story aloud. Recording your stories in this early writing and rehearsal period and listening to them while following the scripts and making necessary changes is useful and recommended.

The script also becomes your reference point every time you go back to the story for review or additional edits. Your script becomes a good place to keep notes: length of story (running time), specific intros, particular actions and movement and comments regarding precise voices and characterizations.

Read the story script aloud over and over until you become extremely familiar with it. A good idea is to memorize dialogue so the words flow easily and believably from your characters. Be prepared to edit your story several times during the rehearsal period. Work with a pencil and mark changes so you can incorporate them when editing the script. Typing your script on a computer is advisable because it cuts down on rewriting and editing time. Write your story to be heard and not to be read. There is a difference. As you type, speak the words aloud using words that are true to your style of telling.

Once you have created a good working script, you can begin the process of blocking your story. "Blocking" is a theatre term which means "adding movement to the script." Even if you choose to have limited movement in your story, you should determine several factors:

- As narrator, where are you standing at the beginning of your story? Remember to "stand in your setting."
- From which direction does your character enter and exit a scene in the story?
- What body position/stance does each character have when conversing?
- What gestures do you wish to use to "paint word pictures?"
- Do you plan to portray any actions such as running in place, climbing, or sword fighting in your storytelling?

Decide where you will stand in your story. As discussed in Chapter 4, *"Live the Story! Stand in Your Setting,"* it's essential to immerse yourself in the story and be in the moment while telling the tale. When you begin the story, be sure to 'see' the scenery of your story's setting before introducing the characters.

Practice, Practice, Practice! Once you are ready to tell your story aloud, practice it over and over again, making necessary edits. You don't need to memorize your script, although you should be extremely familiar with it. Memorize your characters' dialogue. Again, recording your story is quite useful in learning it and helps to determine the story's timing. This is valuable when planning your story sets for a program or if you are requested to perform a tale of a specific length. I always record my stories, including any introduction. Then I transfer them to the computer and burn a CD so I can listen to, and learn, the stories at home and in the car.

C. REFINE

The job of refining, or polishing, your story may seem like a never-ending process. You probably will experiment with, and make changes to, your story numerous times.

Practice 'morphing' and then 'jumping' from one speaking character to another, keeping your characterizations distinct and clear. 'Morphing' is a method I use to teach students how to change, or transform, from one speaking character to another. This is done in slow motion at first as morphing and then speeds up to jumping from character to character.

Exercise: Dialogue, Morphing and Jumping, Oh My!

As an example, let's use the same characters of "Baba Yaga" and "Marina" from Chapter 4 in the scene when they first meet. Baba Yaga faced left to question Marina and Marina faced right to respond to the witch.

- Become evil Baba Yaga, perhaps with your body slumped and bent, with a menacing glare and pointing a crooked finger at the little girl. Facing left as Baba Yaga, ask in a screechy, gravelly voice, *"Vat do you vant, leetle girl?"*

- Now slowly turn your body to face the opposite direction (to the right), as you stand up straight as Marina, hands folded in front, with a nervous gaze, and in a soft, higher pitch innocently reply, *"If you please, my stepmoter vants to borrow a needle und tread."*

- Slowly turn to the left again as you change back to Baba Yaga and cry, *"Und vat vill you do for me?"*

- Again, slowly turn to the right and change/morph into Marina and respond with a curtsy, *"V-v-vatever you vish, Auntie."*

Repeat this sequence several times morphing back and forth from witch to young girl, always crystallizing (manifesting) each character before you transform into the other character. Gradually speed this sequence up so you identify with the ESSENCE of each character: Baba Yaga is evil and untrustworthy. Marina is innocent and vulnerable. Eventually, the morphing turns into a smooth transition allowing you to 'jump' seamlessly back and forth from each character when they converse.

Be sure to quarter turn left and quarter turn right with a simple body/foot rotation. This is done in place, so be careful not to turn your body and walk a few steps before transforming into the characters. By making quarter turns, as opposed to half turns, you avoid standing in profile, thereby allowing your characters to clearly be seen and heard by the audience.

Feedback is vital. Don't be afraid to reach out to the people closest to you – friends, family members, colleagues, coaches, or anyone who knows you and your work – and seek fair and constructive feedback. Practice telling the story as often as you can to someone you trust. Ask for honest, helpful comments, especially on your character interpretations. Do your story characters differ from one another? How would your listeners describe them? Is there any part of the story that doesn't make sense? Can they hear and understand you? Does the story flow? Listen carefully to feedback and suggestions, and write down changes you wish to incorporate in your script.

Take Notes. Keep files of your scripts with edits and feedback comments and include various introductions, or lead-ins, for each story. A story can be introduced in several different ways during more than one season. I keep the running time of each story circled at the top left-hand corner of the script for quick reference when putting together a specific program and need an idea of the total length of the show.

Be Prepared! Take time the day before a performance to review your stories, contract and directions. It helps to look at a map. List the stories you plan to tell. I jot them down on a small post-it note and place the note near my water bottle during performance so I can glance at it when getting a sip of water. After the show, I check off which stories were told and cross off ones not used. Then I place the updated post-it back on the contract before filing it away. This comes in handy when that sponsor books a return visit, so I can see which stories were already told at that location.

Above all, when performing, relax and enjoy the diverse, exciting characters you've created. The audience will appreciate them too!

6. Pathways to the Main Stage

Whenever I find myself standing on stage stark naked and forgetting my lines, it's a relief to discover I'm having a bad dream! Fortunately, neither scenario has occurred in real life partly because my practice is to thoroughly prepare, especially when learning and rehearsing new material. Being PREPARED definitely gives you confidence and keeps nerves and subsequent 'cotton-mouth' at bay regardless of who's in your audience, especially if it's a critic, potential sponsor or one of your peers. There's nothing calming about stepping on stage feeling unprepared and under rehearsed.

However, there's a difference between nervousness due to lack of preparation and having 'butterflies in your stomach.'

Many performers claim to have 'butterflies' before stepping on stage and that can be a good thing. 'Butterflies' means feeling slight anticipation of an upcoming main stage performance or an opening night of a show. Your stomach may feel fluttery, excited and a bit nervous. This experience is often welcomed by professional performers because it can create an adrenaline rush, give you more energy, keep you on your toes and allow your mind to stay sharp.

Next Steps to Becoming a Pro

As experienced performers, we should always look for additional growth opportunities and new ideas to keep our careers on track and take us to the next step in our storytelling livelihood. Set goals for yourself and work at your profession every day. Make a list of these goals and cross them off as you go. At the end of each day, review what you accomplished and which goals get carried over to the next day. If one of your goals is long term, keep it on your list and refer to it frequently for incentive.

It's important to present yourself as a pro in all aspects of your career. My approach to being a Master Story Performer™ begins with the Three C's Approach to Professionalism: be Competent, be Consistent and be Consummate.

A. BE COMPETENT

Get training and grow to be proficient in your storytelling. Improve performance skills with a 'trained trainer,' teacher or director. Work with someone with credentials and expertise in her field. Expand and increase your credentials and accomplishments. Take classes in acting and improvisation to increase performance skills. If you sing in your stories but have never trained with a professional voice teacher, consider studying with one. Review and rehearse your stories until they are polished. Write a little every day or set aside a specific writing time to build your repertoire and increase story lists. When you are hired, deliver what you say you will do or is expected of you. One of your goals should be to attain satisfied customers and earn repeat business.

B. BE CONSISTENT

Be reliable, dependable, and on time. If traveling to a performance, anticipate possible delays and leave early so you arrive with enough time to set up and test the microphone prior to the audience's arrival. Review directions and instructions to avoid getting lost and allow extra time if traveling during rush hour. Bring along your contract with sponsor's contact information so you can call if you run into traffic or your flight is delayed. Great communication is vital. Return phone calls, e-mails, and contracts in a timely manner, thereby establishing trust with your sponsors and associates. Time your stories (including introductions) and exhibit excellent time management skills during performance. Look at a watch or clock from time to time. Be flexible, patient and gracious with your hosts and audiences, as many factors are beyond our control.

C. BE CONSUMMATE

Be the C.P., the Consummate Professional, in everything you do: deliver the complete package with integrity. Advertise what you deliver and always deliver what you advertise. Dress for success. Show respect and gain respect of others especially sponsors, audience members, additional performers, colleagues and technical professionals. Set high standards for yourself and create an outstanding reputation as an accomplished, reliable professional. An excellent reputation, one which ignites others to spread the word about you, is worth more than spending a ton of money on marketing.

Finding Your Niche

What sets you apart from other storytellers? Why should a sponsor hire YOU and not someone else? In an ever-increasing roster of storytellers and performers, you may want to explore your **niche**, or brand. Determine what makes you unique, distinctive and sets you apart from others. Finding your niche is not always easy, especially if your style is a 'jack of all trades' – but a master of none. Do you have a specialty or an area of expertise? Consider your body of work and the type of stories you tell and to which you are drawn. Do you embrace your cultural heritage and represent it in your repertoire? Perhaps you possess a genre/type of story or style of storytelling that makes you matchless from others. Here are two exercises to help find your niche:

Exercise 1: Write a minimum of six adjectives or phrases that describe your storytelling style. Include what others have told you or written about you. Circle the top three adjectives that BEST describe your style.

Exercise 2: In a small group or with a partner, take turns writing a short 'remembrance' about each other focusing on:

- How did that person's storytelling make you feel?
- What do you remember most about that person's performance and what impact did it have on you?

The research you conduct, along with responses from others, may allow you to zero in on identifying what special talents you bring to the table and can assist you in determining better means to market yourself.

I had an 'aha' moment when I participated in the above exercises with a group of storytellers. I discovered new adjectives to better describe my performance style from their feedback. Some of their descriptions resonated with me, so I took them to heart. I quickly incorporated "Latino passion, fire and wit" into my professional profile and marketing pieces.

Have a Presence - Tools to Get You Noticed!

Picture Perfect

Invest in your career by having top quality professional photos taken, and consider purchasing more than one pose. Obtain at least one excellent color head shot which shows your eyes and personality and at least one upper body shot with movement or animation while performing. Having high quality photos on your website and marketing pieces can make a difference and get you noticed by potential sponsors.

Website to Wow

Your website is your biggest calling card. It should look extremely professional and not too busy. It also needs to be effortless to navigate and comprehend. The index (Home page) should represent your personality and style and should include a definition of what you do. Be sure to include one or two professional photos because sponsors want to see what you look like. Having an excellent quote from a newspaper or patron is a bonus. Your website should include:

- Links to your repertoire page listing program and workshop offerings
- Additional photos, head shots and animated body shots
- An electronic press kit
- Samples of your work, including videos and audio links
- Lists of places you've performed
- Quotes from the press and satisfied benefactors
- Product offerings such as recordings, books and DVDs
- Teacher guide or articles you've written and published
- Information on how to contact you
- A calendar/schedule of your upcoming performances

Keep your calendar and website current. Update them often because clients do check, and be certain your links function properly.

Here's My Postcard

In addition to your website, a **hard copy marketing piece** is an invaluable tool. You need a marketing piece to give to sponsors, circulate at conferences, festivals, CD release parties or mass mail to potential customers. Always carry this piece with you to hand out wherever you go. Anyone interested in what you do for a living should receive one. I've met several future sponsors on airplanes because I handed them my colored postcard when they asked me my profession. Be it a brochure, business card, postcard, flyer, demo CD or book – have something 'hard copy' to physically hand to potential clients and contacts. You never know where it will end up, preferably not in the circular file!

For fifteen years, I handed out and mailed an expensive multi-page brochure. After the debut of my first web site, I downsized to a 4" x 6" full color postcard printed with two photos, a terrific quote from the press, a short bio, my contact information and the website URL prominently placed for all to see – and visit. This colorful postcard has successfully served as my hard copy marketing piece for several years.

When I unveiled a new website, I created a matching postcard reflecting this site and including two new professional photos. Always with a hand-written note, this postcard accompanies mailed contracts, CD orders, business correspondence and marketing packages. You can employ a graphic designer to produce your marketing pieces or, as I did, use an online printing company that offers free templates to design postcards and print them in bulk at discounted prices.

Networking, Networking, Cha Cha Cha!

Online networking is another beneficial tool. In addition to being part of several LISTSERVs, I belong to multiple artist directory listings offered for free plus I have a presence on several professional online directories which I purchase and renew every year. Include your photo with the listing. It's worth the extra money, as many sponsors don't take a listing seriously if they can't see an image of the artist.

Social media, such as Facebook, Twitter and LinkedIn, is another excellent way to network, plus it's free and allows networking opportunities with hundreds of professional storytellers, performers and potential customers. It's likely these communication sites will change in time, so stay current with your online presence.

Networking face to face with other professional performing artists is definitely worthwhile as well. Attending storytelling conferences is a valuable investment, and presenting at one is even better. Going to storytelling festivals and professional spoken word events are excellent for meeting and observing national and international performers. Emceeing at these events, and doing a 'sit-up-and-take-notice' job of it, is another way for national tellers, sponsors and festival producers to see the consummate professional in you and make recommendations to others. As emcee, rehearse and memorize the introductions and resist the temptation of reading from a card. Keep in mind that many national tellers are used as a resource by festival producers and directors who are looking for referrals of new talent with an impressive reputation.

Dress to Impress

Looking **polished** takes effort. From combed, neat hair to attractive clothing to clean, unscuffed shoes. Think of this as an investment in you. Plan your outfit the day before a show, soup to nuts, including jewelry, belt, vest, watch, footwear and undergarments. When clothing is laid out the night before, it makes getting ready in the morning easier and less stressful. Select clothing accordingly, depending on the type of microphone you use. If wearing a headset mic, big dangle earrings may swing and hit the headset. If using a lavaliere (lapel) mic, a buttoned shirt, blouse or secure jacket will give the mic clip a place to fasten securely.

I believe in dressing up for any audience, whether telling to three people or three thousand. It's my way of celebrating and honoring them. It never ceases to amaze me how many audience members take notice and comment on my clothing, choice of colors, accessories, and shoes. When performing on a main stage, especially under lighting, consider wearing a bit of makeup such as lipstick or gloss, eyeliner and a touch of translucent powder to reduce a shiny face or bald head. Also, be sure your hair, or hat if you wear one, doesn't cover your eyes or cause shadows on your face. We want to see your expressive eyes.

Programs with Pizazz

Create **well-designed story sets** to wow your audiences. A carefully crafted story set also allows for a smooth flow to the performance. Depending on what type of stories you were hired to perform, plan on opening with something engaging to grab and hold your audience's attention. This could be one of your signature pieces. If your repertoire includes folk tales and personal stories, you might consider performing a combination of the two provided they fit in with the show's theme. After a long story, do a short ditty. After you tell a few humorous tales, add a serious or poignant piece. If you sing well and on key, you may want to sing in the middle of the show or close with a song. Make sure you open and close your performance with strong material. Presenting a diverse program showcases your range, repertoire and multi-talents.

Keep On Your Toes

Audiences can be unpredictable. You should **stay focused** and on your toes, alert and poised at all times. Reading your audience is vital to the success of your performance (see Chapter 7, *"Command Performance"*). Depending upon audience response, you may choose to change your presentation. Plan your program in advance but have extra stories, songs or poems 'in your back pocket' in case you need to switch gears during the show or do an encore. Be flexible and learn to think on your feet, something you can achieve by taking improvisational theatre classes.

Once I performed bilingual stories to a predominantly Spanish-speaking family audience in Cambridge, Massachusetts. The following week, in an effort to foster reading and storytelling in the home, I returned to teach basic storytelling skills to the adult participants. When I arrived to present the workshop, to my surprise, the room was filled with entire families eager to hear *"mas cuentos"* – more stories. Apparently, word had spread throughout the community that *una cuentista*, a storyteller, was in town. All the adults who signed up for the workshop returned with their children and extended families. I quickly changed gears to accommodate their request, utilizing extra stories from my 'back pocket.' I was able to roll with the punches and adjust my program because, being a pro, I had prepared for the unpredictable.

This time, the program was different. We had another story performance, one with an abundance of participation, which taught the attendees basic skills to empower them to share their own stories. It was a win-win.

7. Command Performance

Making the leap to the main stage can be daunting, but we push ourselves to learn, grow and blossom. Through skill-building exercises and experience, you can heighten your performance and gain confidence as a pro when commanding the stage.

In this chapter, we will address several professional behavior techniques including:

- Understanding the Fourth Wall
- The intimacy of storytelling - trust your instincts
- Conducting a tech check - microphones and lighting
- Claiming the stage and welcoming the audience
- Stage Presence
- Reading an audience
- Handling unexpected problems

Frequently, while teaching a storytelling or acting class, I find myself comparing and contrasting the two art forms. I know that a storyteller can incorporate acting techniques into a story. And I know that an actor can incorporate storytelling techniques into a play or theatre piece. But there's a difference between storytelling and theatre. Before you make the leap to the main stage, you should understand and appreciate the differences, especially when learning how to trust yourself enough to connect with your audience and establish a rapport with them often without visual contact.

Understanding the Fourth Wall

An actor, more often than not, performs the scenes of a play on stage behind the **"Fourth Wall,"** yet she is able to sense the audience even though she doesn't have the benefit of seeing their faces. The Fourth Wall is a theatre term referring to the imaginary line, or wall, between the actors on the stage and the audience. The audience observes, or witnesses, the storyline as it unfolds. It's as if the fourth wall of a set (such as the kitchen in *"Death of a Salesman,"* the living room in *"The Odd Couple,"* or the balcony and terrace in *"Romeo and Juliet"*) were cut open and removed, allowing the audience to watch what's going on in the play. Actors on stage speak to each other and interact with one other, while the audience observes. Actors do not turn to the audience and personally draw them into the action of the play by making direct eye contact. They are unable to see individual faces or expressions which can give positive reinforcement.

Most actors don't rely on the audience's laughter and applause to tell them whether or not they are doing a good job. That's not to say that actors don't feel the audience's presence and energy. They can usually "feel" whether the audience is with them or not as if there's an energy field between them.

PAY ATTENTION - Here's the most important element for storytellers to understand and apply: actors must use their intuition and awareness skills to interpret feedback and silent reaction from the audience. The result is plenty of "give and take" between audience and actor without the actor relying on looking into the eyes of the audience. By 'give and take,' I'm referring to what the audience gets from the actor and vice versa, making each performance special and unique.

The Intimacy of Storytelling - Trust Your Instincts

Intimacy is a key part of storytelling. The teller looks into the eyes of the audience and together they tell the story. As the story unfolds, there is no fourth wall when the narrator looks at the audience to include them, letting them in on what's happening, and sharing the excitement of the story. By seeing the audience, the storyteller can gauge how the story is presented. An audience's facial expressions and body language speak volumes to the storyteller, who may edit the story or speed it up, depending on the audience's reactions. Even if the storyteller acts out a dialogue between two or more story characters, those characters often include the audience by looking directly at the listeners during some of the spoken dialogue.

Of course, the narrator can break through such a "scene" in a story by looking at the audience to make a comment, observation, or facial expression before continuing with the narration of the story. There is no fourth wall here. Teller and audience visually share the story, often composing it together as it unfolds. There is 'give and take' and great energy between teller and audience, as in theatre. But what happens when the auditorium is dark and the storyteller cannot rely on seeing faces in the audience due to bright stage lights? She must rely on her instincts and intuition, just as an actor does in a play.

Exercise #1: Tapping Into Your Intuition

For the next five minutes, lay flat on your back, arms resting by your sides, and eyes closed. Relax, slowly inhaling through the nose and exhaling through the mouth. With every inhale and exhale, release tension and relax muscles. Starting at the top of your head, slowly inhale and exhale, traveling down to your face and neck, followed by shoulders, arms, hands and fingers, back and chest, hips, thighs, legs, feet and toes. Keep your eyes closed, and tune into the room. Be aware of your surroundings. Listen carefully to sounds you may hear.

Afterwards, slowly sit up and answer these questions. What sounds did you hear? Did you sense someone quietly entering the room? Were you focused or distracted by unexpected noise and commotion? Did you get sidetracked by going through your laundry list or were you tuned into your body and centered?

Tapping into your insight, intuition and perception abilities allows you to sense your audience and read them more accurately. This plays a significant role in developing stage presence.

Next is an excellent improvisational theatre game to help fine tune your skills in becoming more aware of your audience, especially if you're unable to see their faces and determine their body language.

Exercise #2: Mirror Image, Give and Take

You will need a partner for this exercise. If you have four to six participants, even better. The group pairs up and faces each other looking into each other's eyes and remains silent. Each pair has a Leader and a Follower, which should be determined by instinct and not discussion. The Leader has the "power" and silently begins the exercise by moving arms and body slow enough for the Follower to imitate exactly, as if looking in a mirror. After a while, the "power" is non-verbally passed from Leader to Follower (the Follower takes over), and their roles are switched. After three minutes of passing the power back and forth between Leader and Follower, each couple stops the exercise and changes partners. After two times with different partners, "Mirror Image" is performed with movement and vocal sounds.

This exercise develops concentration, coordination and cooperation. It enhances awareness to read or gauge an audience. It teaches participants how to "give and take" when performing and how to improvise and trust your instincts when interacting with an audience and inviting audience participation.

Conducting a Tech Check - Microphones and Lighting

Prior to a professional main stage performance in a theatre, auditorium, festival stage or huge outdoor venue, the sound and lighting engineers will invite you to a technical check, in order to test your microphone levels and determine if any special lighting is necessary. Conducting a proper tech check ensures a smooth performance, avoiding poor audio and other technical issues. The sound engineer often contacts you in advance to find out what type of microphone you prefer to use.

Microphones come in a variety of different types including:

- A vocal/presenter corded mic on a traditional or boom stand
- A hand-held wireless mic that can also be placed on a stand
- A wireless lavaliere, or lapel, mic which clips several inches below your chin onto your clothing and the body pack clips on the back of your belt or skirt

- A wireless headset, the base of which attaches around your ear or back of the head and the body pack clips on the back of your clothing

Select and use the type of microphone to best showcase your voice and style of performing.

When festival producers ask in advance what type of microphone I require, I request a headset or lapel microphone because I prefer a hands-free mic during performance. If they inform me that only a corded mic on a traditional stand or a handheld wireless mic are available, I tell them I'll bring my wireless system and headset mic with me. I also offer to speak in advance with their sound engineer regarding my equipment and any concerns he may have. This way I am assured that during the show I'll be able to have 'hands-freedom.'

To conduct a proper tech check, stand center stage facing the audience. When the sound engineer signals you to begin speaking, respond with *"Testing, testing. One, two, three."* Never blow on a microphone or tap your hand on a mic to see if it's live! This is harmful to the sensitive equipment. Wait until the engineer gives you the cue to speak because he will turn on your mic beforehand and begin making adjustments to the sound levels. If he says *"Keep speaking,"* be sure to use phrases from an actual story you plan to tell, from the loudest part of your tale to the softest. If you intend to sing during your presentation, definitely sing a little bit so the engineer can adjust the sound board appropriately.

Don't make the mistake of assuming the microphone replaces your need to project your voice on stage. 'Chicago' rules still apply (see Chapter 3). I've seen nationally known entertainers on festival stages where they spoke with less than supported voices, apparently assuming the mics will do the projecting for them. They clearly didn't test their true range of volume, or lack of, during tech checks, resulting in uneven and often muffled sound. The audiences had difficulty following their storylines and subsequently didn't respond to the performances as anticipated.

When performing under the lights, you most likely won't be able to see the faces in your audience. Often you're lucky to see the outlines of their bodies. Don't let this darkness throw you off your game. Prepare for this by expecting that the audience will be in the dark, and you most likely will have bright lights in your eyes. If so, try not to squint or comment that you can't see anything – that could make your audience feel awkward. Pretend you CAN see them. Relax, smile and welcome your audience. Again, trust your instincts.

If you are accustomed to seeing your audience's faces during an interactive portion of your performance, you may not have the opportunity to request that house lights be turned up to 60-80% full. Most audience members aren't comfortable or relaxed watching a main stage performance with bright house lights on. However, during your lighting check, you could ask the lighting technician if it's possible to raise/lower house lights during your performance. Or you may decide to go with the flow and leave the lighting design as is.

Completing a sound and lighting check (a tech check) not only ensures that your voice will be heard by all, but it should build confidence and give you peace of mind that you will be awesome in performance. It also helps keep nerves at bay later on when you enter the stage to greet the live audience.

Claiming the Stage and Welcoming the Audience

If you don't have the chance to be on stage during a tech check, make sure you enter the room and step on stage PRIOR to your live performance. Take the opportunity to explore the stage before the house opens. Walk to center stage and look out into the audience. Take in the whole auditorium, as you scan your eyes from the left, to center, to the right. Take several deep breaths. Envision people sitting in those empty chairs anxious to hear your tales. This is vital in relieving anxiety or nerves. Later, when it's time for your performance and you enter the stage, you will have already claimed the stage earlier in the day. You will have more confidence knowing you are not brand new to this space and you will start to feel as if you own the stage.

At the live performance, before you enter the stage to begin speaking, change your focus from worries and nerves to your passion and excitement for the stories you're about to tell the audience. Think of it as, *"I've got some fantastic stories to share and I can't wait until you hear them!"* There isn't a single story in my repertoire that I don't love and consider a personal favorite.

When you enter the main stage, do it with confidence and skill **as a pro**. Walk to center stage and make it your own. Look out to the audience, smile and look pleasant. If the stage lighting is bright, preventing you from seeing the audience, pretend you can see their faces. Say something to make the audience feel welcome, such as *"Good evening! Thanks for coming,"* or *"Hello! I'm so happy to be here,"* or *"Welcome! It's great to see you!"* Show your human side. If someone introduced you, there's no need to restate your name, but if you were not introduced – or your name was mispronounced - it's a good idea to include your name as well without making it sound as if you're correcting the emcee. Be cheerful, sincere and compelling enough to grab the audience's attention and establish a rapport with them. Think of this as a hearty handshake with someone you're interested in knowing.

Making the audience feel welcome helps to establish a relationship with them – and gives them a chance to see who you are. This should be done efficiently to establish a mutual connection.

Confidence is key, but leave your ego at the door. The most effective way to engage your audience is not with a barrage of rambling introductions. Don't fall into the trap of overdoing it – chatting on and on with the audience, "feeling the love," and before you know it, you've used up most of your time! It's all about building a connection quickly. You want the audience to feel relaxed and enjoy your performance. They are there not to judge, but to have a great time. They are in your corner.

Stage Presence

To command a room, you need to give the instant impression of being on top of the world. When you combine confidence, competence, and charisma as you claim the stage and begin your program, you should be "in the Zone" and ready to captivate and command the audience. You want to create a connection based on mutual values and common emotions that fosters trust between you and the audience. It's important to immerse yourself in the story and be in the moment while telling the tale. Knowing your stories cold (rehearse, rehearse, rehearse!) will give you the confidence to focus on the audience and not on your memory. Keep in mind your goal/motive for telling stories. As a people person, one of my goals is to show the audience a good time hoping they leave having had a memorable experience. If they learned something, that's icing on the cake. Nothing motivates and satisfies me more than experiencing palpable energy emanating from the audience when on stage and in the moment.

If you sense that you're losing impact while speaking, it could be that you're babbling a little too much. Perhaps your introduction is going on and on. It is easy to sense this, especially if you see bored faces or don't hear anticipated reactions from the audience. This means it's time to get on with the story and pick up the pace. If most of your storytelling is humorous, you may want to show another side of your personality. Tell a more serious or poignant story or give an emotional or vulnerable introduction to the next story. Be yourself and keep it authentic.

Reading an Audience

Sometimes when observing your audience, you may see a raised eyebrow or confused expression on several people's faces. That may be a sign you are speaking too fast or a particular part of the story is confusing. If that's the case, you may want to slow it down and speak more clearly, or you may want to adapt your story by explaining something that may be unclear to the audience. If you see an audience member sitting with arms crossed in front of the chest and a stern expression on the face, this doesn't necessarily mean that person is not enjoying what you're saying. It could simply be that he is listening intently.

If you are unable to see your audience's expressions due to bright stage lights, and they are quiet when you anticipate a vocal reaction, you may want to either clarify that part of the story or adjust your pace. Depending on the type of story you're telling, you may choose to engage the audience by asking a question: *"Has that ever happened to you?"* or *"So what do you think Coyote did next?"* This involves thinking on your toes to help read your audience when you're unable to see them. Most likely, your audience will verbally respond, allowing you to react accordingly and make adjustments as needed.

Often I am hired to perform Latino bilingual stories. The amount of Spanish included in performance depends upon individual audiences and their reactions. Although the Spanish is always translated into English, for all to understand, I strive to sense how much (or how little) the audience will allow. Reading a predominantly non-Latino audience is always a small challenge. Often I test the audience to see how open it is to learning and speaking some Spanish throughout the performance. If I enter the stage and cry, *"¡Hola! ¡Buenos* dias!", and the audience echoes this phrase in return, I will try the next test by asking, "¿Como estan ustedes? How are you?" If I hear, "Muy bien y tu?" (Very well and you?), I know I can proceed with as much español (and English translations) as I feel each story warrants, while being careful not to speak too rapidly. Storytelling festival-goers and collegiate audiences appreciate the bilingual storytelling the most, and many have expressed their preference for my reciting the Spanish words and phrases first, followed by the English translation, enabling them to test their own knowledge of the Spanish language.

However, once in a while after a performance, an audience member complains that the show contained too much Spanish, stating a preference for hearing the stories in English only. During an evening performance, I overheard a man mumble to his wife, "I didn't come here to learn Spanish." But I was equally surprised with her response, "¡Shhh – silencio, hush!" Fortunately, the majority of audience feedback is positive when I incorporate both languages in the Latino stories.

Handling Unexpected Problems

A storytelling performance is a live event, so unforeseen glitches can be inevitable. Technical difficulties may occur by sound issues or lighting problems and distractions from the audience can be disconcerting. The best way to handle these issues is with grace and positive energy. If it's a technical issue, remember the adage: *"The show must go on!"* Unless the stage manager or a technical person comes to the stage and tells you to stop, keep going. If it's a phone ringing in the audience, try to ignore it, especially if you're in the middle of a story. If this happens during an intro, you may choose to ignore it or make a simple joke about it and move on. However, if someone in the audience collapses, and the audience reacts to it, you may want to stop until the incident is cleared. Again, trust your instincts, be a leader, and try to make the audience feel calm and comfortable again.

Sometimes one cannot avoid performance anxiety, no matter how prepared. Years ago, I performed at Gimistory – The Cayman Islands International Storytelling Festival. On "Dupy" (Ghost) Night, the show was held on a beach underneath a grove of palm trees. It was a dark evening, as the moon danced beneath clouds and soft ocean waves offered background music. The large audience nestled together in anticipation and dread. The setting was ideal, as the chilling stories began to unfold.

I was scheduled last and waited offstage in the shadows. The wireless lavaliere microphone was hidden beneath my long, black velvet cape. As the emcee finished her introduction, I turned on the body pack and stepped up on the wooden platform. At that moment, lightening flashed and booming thunder rumbled overhead. I thought, *"Oh, dear*

God." The Caymanians cheered as if I had arranged it, and then the skies opened up with torrential rainfall. The Caymanians cheered louder, as they covered their heads with plastic bags and jackets ready to listen. I was anxious about being on stage in a thunderstorm with a live microphone attached to my bosom, but the audio technician and festival director nodded with a 'thumbs up' to proceed. I pictured next day's headlines: "American Storyteller Dies Mid-sentence from Lightning Bolt. Audience Cheers."

Then I remembered the 'Words of Wisdom' learned years ago from theatre professors: *"The show must go on, no matter what!"* So I sucked it up, wiped the rain from my eyes, and performed the scariest story I knew, one I wrote about the Jersey Devil, and frightened the you-know-what out of the Caymanians - and lived to tell about it.

Here are two anecdotes about audience connection and being human.

I was performing at a festival in Chicago, and as I took the stage in the huge theatre, I felt moisture gathering in my right nostril. Knowing my lavaliere microphone was live, I sniffed quietly and continued with my story introduction. By the next sentence, the moisture increased. A runny nose? Where did this come from? I sniffed again and casually brushed my finger over the nostril and continued. A quick glance at my finger and over to the emcee (who was frantically rooting through her pocketbook for a tissue) confirmed my worst nightmare. It was red. I was having a nosebleed on stage for no apparent reason. I was mortified. Just then the nostril gave way and the drip headed south. One more wipe with my knuckle, and a shrug from the emcee announcing she'd come up empty, I turned to the audience for assistance. *"Does anyone have a tissue please? It appears I'm having a small nosebleed."* Two women, already on the case, waved Kleenex. The closest one hurried to the stage to save me. I quickly wiped and sniffed simultaneously, as I glanced at the ASL interpreter, who was signing "nosebleed" with big gestures not to be misunderstood.

The audience looked quite concerned. I smiled and said, *"Thank you for your patience. I'm sorry, I never get nosebleeds. Perhaps this is caused by the difference in altitude or...menopause?"* We all had a good laugh, to my relief. After urging the audience not to spend the rest of the performance staring at my nostrils, the show went on without further interruption. My nose behaved itself.

Another time, I was invited to perform at a seaport aquarium. When I arrived, the sponsor informed me I would be storytelling in the Dolphin Theatre. When I entered the auditorium, hoping to see the two dolphins, the trainer explained that during my show they wouldn't be swimming in the large pool behind me, as they normally do. Instead, they were safe and resting in a small pool behind an underwater gate.

The audience arrived and sat in the theatre seats facing me, and I stood on the narrow platform in front of the large swimming pool. Everyone was excited, because this was the aquarium's first time having a storyteller in Dolphin Theatre. I began performing an ocean story about a young boy who lived in a seaport town. When I got to the part where the boy walked along a sandy shore and spotted some slick black seals, I imitated the sounds of barking seals. I continued narrating until I got to the part of the story where a large flock of sea gulls flies overhead. I gestured up to the sky and created a repetition of excited sea gull calls. All of a sudden, I heard another noise coming from behind me. I swung around, and there was Misty the Dolphin bobbing up and down to the call of the sea gulls! Then she rose up on her tail and danced backwards with her voiced reply. Apparently, when Misty heard the sounds of ocean life, she jumped over the gate and swam over to say *"Hello."*

The audience was as surprised as I and began calling to the dolphin. I quickly acknowledged Misty and incorporated her into the story. I told the audience the young boy was so pleased by the dolphin's dance he applauded her (as did the audience), and continued on his journey. By now, the dolphin trainer had blown his whistle to retrieve Misty, and I finished the story to everyone's delight, especially mine. I may never have the opportunity to swim with dolphins, but I'll never forget my charming experience of storytelling with one.

8. Take a Bow and Final Thoughts

Kudos to you for a compelling, humorous and heartfelt performance! You took the stage by storm and successfully connected with the audience. You made each listener feel as if you were speaking directly to them.

Savor your moment in the spotlight. Be sure to graciously accept the audience's applause with a nod or a bow. Show your appreciation and thank them for attending. If time allows, mention where you'll be performing next.

If another performer is scheduled to appear after you, be respectful and vacate the stage. If an audience member approaches you to chat, take the conversation away from the stage to allow the stage and technical crews to set up for the next performance. Be the consummate professional and others will notice.

In closing, I'd like to share my "Words of Wisdom." As a performer, be true to YOU. Don't imitate anyone else's style, and don't use any other teller's work without permission. Write and perform your own stories, original or adapted, with your personality in words you normally use. Be as honest as you can especially when presenting something poignant or humorous. Try not to laugh at your own jokes unless the audience laughs first. Allow the audience to see the real you. Be yourself. But be on time.

When performing, it's not about you and your ego. It's about your audience. Their comfort level and ability to see and hear you, trusting you enough to travel the story journey with you, are paramount. Please continue to learn and grow as a performer. *"¡Vive el Cuento!* Live the Story!"

9. About the Author

With a face and voice that launched a thousand characters, **Leeny Del Seamonds, Master Story Performer™**, is an internationally acclaimed performer, coach, and multi award-winning recording artist. A dedicated Teaching Artist with a BA in Theatre/Performing Arts (*magna cum laude*), Leeny's animated, uplifting tales and tunes reflect her love of people and desire to embrace life to its fullest. From a prized television show to a village in China, to the Comix Club in NYC to the National Storytelling Festival and Cayman Islands International Festival, Leeny encourages listeners to rejoice in human and cultural diversity, inviting them to share in her Cuban-American sense of humor and joy of performing. With Latino passion, fire and wit, Leeny's dynamic one-woman shows and renowned workshops headline happenings worldwide.

Find her web site at:
http://www.LeenyDelSeamonds.com
Twitter her @leenydels

Made in the USA
Middletown, DE
31 March 2015